They Shall Be Saved

By Christopher K. Turney

They Shall Be Saved
© 2025 Christopher K. Turney
All rights reserved.

No part of this publication may be reproduced, stored in a retrieval system, or transmitted in any form or by any means, electronic, mechanical, photocopying, recording, or otherwise, without the prior written permission of the author, except for brief quotations used in reviews or scholarly works.

ISBN: 979-8-218-80268-4

For permissions, inquiries, or additional resources, please contact:
Christopher K. Turney
Kingdom Reign Ministries

Chris@krmchurch.com
Scripture quotations are used by permission and credited accordingly on the following page.

Scripture Credits:

Unless otherwise noted, Scripture quotations are from the New King James Version® (NKJV), © 1982 by Thomas Nelson. Used by permission. All rights reserved.

Additional Scripture references may include translations such as:

- New International Version® (NIV), © 1973, 1978, 1984, 2011 by Biblica, Inc.™

- English Standard Version® (ESV), © 2001 by Crossway Bibles, a publishing ministry of Good News Publishers.

Dedication

To all who hunger for the fullness of salvation, not just as an escape from death, but as a return to divine purpose, sonship, and the eternal blessing spoken over them before time began.

You were known, chosen, and loved in Christ from the foundation of the world.

Table of Contents

Foreword 1

Preface 3

Introduction 7

Chapter 1: Why Salvation Is Necessary 9

Chapter 2: Born Again, A Change of Citizenship 17

Chapter 3: The Significance of the Lamb 27

Chapter 4: Identity Over Destination 37

Chapter 5: Kingdom Salvation 47

Chapter 6: The Power and Permanence of Redemption .. 55

Chapter 7: Restored to Our Origin 61

Chapter 8: Living as the Redeemed 71

Chapter 9: The Adam Exchange 77

Chapter 10: Saved by Grace 85

Chapter 11: Baptized into Christ 93

Foreword

I have had the privilege of knowing Apostle Chris Turney for over three decades. His exceptional ability to articulate the Gospel in a clear and accessible way is truly a gift. This book, born from his desire to help people experience God's presence, promises to be a transformative read for both believers and those seeking faith.

Apostle Chris masterfully presents the Gospel, making it understandable for everyone while emphasizing the importance of salvation and our identity. For believers, this book addresses the core of who they are, and for those new to faith, it provides a clear path to understanding. Apostle Chris's insights into the Kingdom of God are shared in a compelling manner, encouraging readers to continue their journey of discovery. He illuminates the concept of heavenly citizenship, demonstrating how our identity shapes our actions rather than the other way around.

This book is suitable for all ages and can be used for personal reflection, teaching, or group discussions. Thank you, Chris, for reminding us of the importance of our identity.

Cruz Bello

Preface

I wrote this book because salvation has been reduced in far too many hearts to a moment instead of a movement, a ticket instead of a transformation. For years, I watched people walk to the altar, say a prayer, and leave unsure if anything really changed. I've sat with sincere believers who loved God but lived with constant fear, wondering if they had truly been saved, if they could lose it, or if they were ever worthy of it to begin with. I wrote They Shall Be Saved to settle the question, not with opinion, but with Scripture.

This book was born out of my own search for clarity. As a pastor, teacher, and son of God, I needed to understand not only what salvation is, but why it is so unshakable. What I found was a revelation that reshaped my message forever: salvation is not just a rescue plan, it's a restoration project. It's not just deliverance from sin, it's entrance into sonship. It's not a backup strategy, it's God's original intention.

They Shall Be Saved walks through the doctrine of salvation as more than a reaction to man's fall. It is the unfolding of God's eternal purpose, to bring many sons to glory, through Christ, by grace. This book confronts popular myths, clarifies tough questions, and most importantly, exalts the finished work of Jesus.

Each chapter takes the reader deeper, from understanding the necessity of being born again to the eternal nature of redemption, the permanence of salvation, and what it means to be united with Christ Himself. My goal is that by the end of this book, you will not only know you are saved, but you will live like one who is redeemed, sealed, and sent.

This book is for the unsure. For the settled. For the student. For the seeker. For the one who has grown up in church and the one who just met Jesus yesterday. I wrote it because salvation is not fragile. It is finished.

They shall be saved.

Because He came. Because He bled. Because He rose.

And because He never fails.

Christopher Turney
Author & Founder, Kingdom Reign Ministries

"Salvation is not a reward for the righteous, it is a gift for the guilty."

— **Steve Lawson**

Introduction

Salvation is one of the most familiar words in the Christian world, and yet, it is often one of the most misunderstood.

For many, salvation is reduced to a moment: a prayer at an altar, a decision card signed, or an emotional response to a sermon.

For others, it is seen only as a destination: escaping hell and securing a place in heaven. But salvation, as revealed in Scripture, is so much more.

This book, They Shall Be Saved, is a journey into the depths and dimensions of God's saving work. We will explore salvation not just as rescue, but as restoration; not just as escape, but as transformation; not just as forgiveness, but as the re-creation of sons and daughters into the likeness of Christ.

Why is salvation necessary?

What does it mean to be born again? How powerful is the blood of the Lamb? What is the significance of the Kingdom in our salvation? Can we lose what we didn't earn? And what does it look like to live as the redeemed today?

These are the questions this book will address, not as abstract doctrines, but as living truths that shape our identity, our families, our churches our communities, and our purpose.

My prayer is that as you walk through these chapters, you will encounter the breathtaking reality of God's saving grace, a salvation that reaches back to the foundation of the world, stretches forward into eternity, and transforms every moment in between.

They shall be saved, not by works, not by striving, but by the finished work of the Lamb.

Let's begin.

Chapter 1
Why Salvation Is Necessary

From the very beginning, God created mankind not merely to exist, but to reflect His image, steward His creation, and walk in intimate fellowship with Him (Genesis 1:26–27). Humanity was meant to be God's representatives on earth, His royal sons and daughters, carrying His nature, His authority, and His purposes. But something happened that fractured this original design.

Sin entered.

And with it came death, separation, and loss.

Romans 5:12 says, *"Therefore, just as through one man sin entered the world, and death through sin, and thus death spread to all men, because all sinned..."* This verse reveals a sobering truth: we are not merely people who make occasional mistakes; we are part of a broken race, cut off from the life of God, infected with death.

We were not **just bad**, we **were dead** (Ephesians 2:1–5).

We were not just **guilty**, we were **enslaved** (Romans 6:16–20).

We were not just **weak**, we were **powerless** (Romans 5:6).

When Adam sinned, several critical things were lost:
- **Fellowship with God** (Genesis 3:8–10):
Adam and Eve hid themselves;
their open communion was ruptured.
- **Authority and dominion** (Genesis 1:28;
Psalm 8:4–6): The earth was placed under the curse;
man lost his ruling position.
- **Purity and wholeness** (Romans 7:18–20):
Sin took root not just in actions but in human nature.
- **Eternal life** (Romans 6:23): Adam and Eve were
barred from the tree of life;
mortality entered the human experience.

What was lost had to be restored, and it would take the prefect sacrifice to bring salvation to man.

Humanity's attempts to save itself have always failed.
- Moral effort falls short because dead people cannot reform themselves.
- Religious rituals cannot bridge the gap between death and life.
- World philosophies offer no answer for sin's penalty.

Ephesians 2:1–5 makes it clear: We were dead in trespasses and sins, following the course of the world, under the influence of the prince of the power of the air.

Salvation had to come from outside, because the dead cannot raise themselves.

God's answer was not a **new system**, a **new law**, or a **new philosophy**. His answer was a **Person — Jesus Christ.**

Jesus came:
- To rescue us from sin's penalty (Romans 6:23)
- To break sin's power over us (Romans 6:14)
- To restore relationship with the Father (2 Corinthians 5:18–19)
- To give us a new identity (2 Corinthians 5:17)
- To secure our future eternally (John 10:28–29)

Salvation is God's comprehensive plan to undo Adam's fall, destroy sin's grip, and restore us to our original purpose.

Many believers see salvation merely as God forgiving our personal sins. But it is much bigger:
- It is God transferring us from Adam's fallen line to Christ's redeemed family.
- It is God making dead people alive.
- It is God reintroducing us to the glory we were created for.

Romans 5:17 says, *"For if by the one man's offense death reigned through the one, much more those who receive abundance of grace and of the gift of righteousness will reign in life through the One, Jesus Christ."*

Without salvation, every human being remains:
- Bound to sin's consequences (Romans 3:23)
- Under judgment (John 3:18–19)
- Without hope (Ephesians 2:12)
- Destined for eternal separation from God
(2 Thessalonians 1:9)

This is why salvation is not optional or secondary, it is the single greatest need of every person, every family, every nation.

Understanding why salvation is necessary helps us see the magnitude of God's gift. Salvation is not just about **fixing bad habits** or **managing guilt.** It is about God restoring humanity to Himself, reviving what was dead, and fulfilling His eternal purposes in Christ for us.

We were not just **slightly flawed**,
We were **fatally ruined**.
We were not just **misguided**, we were **lost**.
We were not just **wounded,** we were **perishing**.
And in Christ, we are **not just improved**,
we are **made new**.

Closing Declaration:
"I was not just lost, I was dead in my sins."
"I was not just weak, I was powerless to live."

"But now, by grace, I am alive forevermore."
"I am restored, redeemed, renewed and resurrected."
"Salvation has brought me home."

Reflection Questions

1. What does Genesis 1:26–27 reveal about God's original intention for humanity? How does this affect how you view yourself today?

2. Romans 5:12 and Ephesians 2:1–5 describe humanity as dead in sin, not just flawed. Why is it important to understand this distinction?

3. How have you seen the effects of Adam's fall (loss of fellowship, authority, purity, and life) play out in your own life or the world around you?

4. Why can't moral effort, religion, or philosophy save us? What does this teach you about the source of true salvation?

5. How does understanding Jesus as the solution, not a system or strategy, reshape your view of Christianity?

6. Which of the reasons Jesus came (rescue, break sin's power, restore relationship, give identity, secure your future) speaks most to you personally right now? Why?

7. Romans 5:17 says we can "reign in life" through Christ. What might that look like practically in your daily life?

8. How does seeing salvation as restoration to God's original purpose (not just forgiveness) shift your understanding of what it means to be saved?

9. Do you see salvation as a one-time event or an ongoing transformation? How do the Scriptures in this chapter help answer that question?

10. What areas of your life still feel "lost, powerless, or dead"? How does the truth of salvation invite you to live fully alive in Christ?

Chapter 2
Born Again, A Change of Citizenship

When Nicodemus came to Jesus by night (John 3), he was a respected teacher of Israel, steeped in the Law, the Prophets, and the religious traditions. But Jesus immediately startled him with these words: "Unless one is born again, he cannot see the kingdom of God" (John 3:3).

This wasn't a call to moral improvement.
This was a call to **rebirth**, a change not just of behavior, but of nature, family, and citizenship.

Nicodemus acknowledged the miracles:

John 3:1-2 (NKJV) says *"Rabbi, we know that You are a teacher come from God; for no one can do these signs that You do unless God is with him."*

But Jesus pointed beyond the signs to substance, beyond miracles to the government behind them…the Kingdom.

Nicodemus is saying:
*"We've **seen** all of the amazing miracles you've done."*
"We know You must be connected to God."

But Jesus immediately replies:
"Unless one is born again, he cannot see the Kingdom…" (John 3:3)

Why? Because **Nicodemus saw the effects** of the Kingdom but couldn't see the **essence** of it.

He saw signs, but not the **government** behind them, the Kingdom

Key truth: *You can see miracles and still miss the King. You can feel power and still not perceive the government behind it.*

Jesus wasn't impressed by Nicodemus' religious credentials. He revealed that no one, not even a Pharisee, can see or enter the Kingdom without being born from above.

Jesus makes a twofold statement:
- "Unless one is born again, he cannot **see** the Kingdom…" (John 3:3)
- "Unless one is born of water and the Spirit, he cannot **enter** the Kingdom…" (John 3:5)
To see = spiritual perception, awareness.
To enter = possession, citizenship, inheritance.

Nicodemus saw the **miracles** but not the **Kingdom**. He acknowledged God was with Jesus, but didn't see **Jesus as the King** of a different domain.

"You've seen the power, Nicodemus. But if you want access to the government behind it, you must be born into it.

John 3:8 (NKJV) says: *"The wind blows where it wishes, and you hear the sound of it, but cannot tell where it comes from and where it goes. So is everyone who is born of the Spirit."*

Jesus is saying:
- You **hear** it (effect),
- But you **don't know** its origin or destination (Kingdom source).
- That's what it's like to see the **influence of God** but **not perceive His Kingdom**.

Nicodemus, like many today, was standing in the **breeze of divine power**, yet **blind to the Kingdom it came from.**

This speaks to the dangers of seeking the signs and wonders. The masses could be witnessing the signs, and yet completely unaware of the government which produced them. Jesus would heal and say "Go and tell no one."

Why? Because He wanted them to seek His Kingdom first (Matthew 6:33), so they could see beyond the miracle to the source of the miracle. To see that source, one must be born again. Born again is not about going to heaven, it is about seeing and entering the Kingdom.

You don't **join** a Kingdom. You don't **work your way in**. You must be **born into it**.

John 1:12–13 (NKJV): *"But as many as received Him, to them He gave the right to become children of God... who were born... of God."*

This not about joining a movement or improving moral standing.

It's about being born into God's household, a spiritual rebirth, a relocation of citizenship.

Change of Citizenship
Philippians 3:20 says *"For our citizenship is in heaven..."*
Colossians 1:13 says *"He has delivered us from the power of darkness and conveyed un into the kingdom of the Son of His love."*

Every true Kingdom grants citizenship by **birthright**. Being born again isn't about fixing your behavior; it's about **changing your bloodline.**

1 Corinthians 15:22 (NKJV): *"As in Adam all die, even so in Christ all shall be made alive."*

Colossians 1:13: *"He has delivered us from the power of darkness and conveyed us into the Kingdom of the Son of His love."*

THEY SHALL BE SAVED

This is not about one ethnicity, denomination, or nation, it is the universal call to be **reborn under a new Father, a new government, and a new citizenship.**

When you are born again, you receive:
- A **new Father** (John 1:13)
- A **new nature** (2 Corinthians 5:17)
- A **new citizenship** (Philippians 3:20)
- A **new inheritance** (Romans 8:17)
- A **new authority** (Luke 10:19)

You no longer live **from earth up**, but **from the Kingdom down**.

"You must be born again." (John 3:7)

You may have seen miracles, heard truth, even felt God's presence… But unless you are born into the Kingdom, you don't have access to the King's reign.

The rebirth is not something we accomplish by works, law, or human will.
It is a gift, a divine work of grace

You are not born into the Kingdom because of:
- Human decision
- Lineage or background
- Personal achievements

You are born again because **God draws, regenerates, and recreates you.**

Being born again means:
-You no longer live under the earth's broken systems; you live under heaven's government
-You no longer strive for worthiness; you live from adoption.
-You no longer represent yourself; you represent your King.

Closing Declaration:
"I wasn't just saved, I was born into royalty.
I wasn't just changed, I was reborn with citizenship.
I don't live under darkness, I live under a King.
I am not an orphan, I am a son.
I am not guessing, I am governed.
I was born into the Kingdom!"

Reflection Questions

1. Why do you think Jesus bypassed Nicodemus' religious status and spoke directly about being "born again"? What does that tell you about salvation?

2. In what ways do you think people today, like Nicodemus, can witness miracles yet miss the Kingdom behind them? Have you ever done that yourself?

3. Jesus said, "Unless one is born again, he cannot see the Kingdom." How does this challenge the idea that Christianity is just about moral improvement or behavior change?

4. What does it mean to be "born of water and the Spirit"? How does this differ from religious rituals or moral effort?

5. John 3:8 compares those born of the Spirit to the wind — unseen origin and direction. How does this analogy help you understand the spiritual nature of Kingdom birth?

6. Reflect on Philippians 3:20 and Colossians 1:13. How does realizing your citizenship is in heaven change how you view your identity, decisions, or daily life?

7. According to this chapter, what are the key things you receive when you're born again (e.g., Father, nature, authority)? Which of these are most impactful to you right now?

8. How is being born again different from joining a church, a movement, or making a decision to improve morally? Why is this distinction important?

9. How does understanding salvation as a rebirth into a new government (not just forgiveness) help reframe your faith walk?

10. What does it mean to no longer be an orphan, but a son? In what ways have you lived like an orphan, and how can you begin to live from sonship and Kingdom authority?

"Jesus didn't come to make bad people good. He came to make dead people alive."

— **Ravi Zacharias**

Chapter 3
The Significance of the Lamb

From the earliest pages of Scripture, the Lamb takes center stage in God's redemptive plan.

In Exodus, God commanded each Israelite household to sacrifice a spotless lamb and apply its blood to the doorposts (Exodus 12:3–7, 12–13).

But here's the critical revelation, and it's one many miss: The blood on the doorpost didn't function like a magical forcefield. It wasn't signaling to the , death angel, *"You can't come in here."* It was declaring something much more profound:

"The firstborn in this house has already died."

According to God's decree, death was coming for the firstborn in every house, Egyptian or Israelite. But God made a provision: A substitute could stand in place of the firstborn.

The lamb became the legal substitute, absorbing the judgment due.

Its blood on the doorpost was not a magical barrier but a **public legal declaration.**

"Death your claim here has already been satisfied. There is no debt left to collect."

This is why Exodus 12:23 says, *"The Lord will pass over the door and not allow the destroyer to come into your house to strike you"*

The destroyer did not pass over because the family was righteous, moral, or good.

The destroyer passed over because **death had already occurred** in that house, the lamb's death.

It wasn't the **absence** of death that saved them, it was the **presence** of substitutionary death.

This foreshadows the gospel in profound ways. When Jesus, the perfect Lamb of God, shed His blood, He satisfied the claims of death **once and for all.**

- Not by blocking death
- Not by magically warding it off
- But stepping into death Himself, as our substitute.

Hebrews 9:22 says, *"Without the shedding of blood there is no remission."*

Why? Because sin's wage is death (Romans 6:23), and only a death can answer a death.

Only a perfect Lamb can answer perfectly for sinners.

THEY SHALL BE SAVED

On the annual Day of Atonement (Yom Kippur), the holiest day in Israels calendar, the high priest would enter the Most Holy place to make atonement for the sins of the people (Leviticus 16).

What's crucial to understand is this:

The focus was not on the people's moral worthiness or even the priest's personal perfection.
The spotlight was entirely on the lamb or sacrificial animals brought before the Lord.

The Lamb Without Blemish
- Exodus 12:5 — "Your lamb shall be without blemish, a male of the first year."
- Leviticus 16:6–10, 15–16 — detailed instructions for the sin offerings and the scapegoat.
- Exodus 29:38–39 — the daily offerings had to be without blemish.

Why such emphasis on without blemish"?
Because the substitute had to be **perfect** to stand in the place of the imperfect.

Any flaw or imperfection in the offering invalidated the atonement.

The people's impurity wasn't the focus, **the offering's purity was**.

This is a profound and liberating truth:

The people's standing before God was not secured by their own righteousness, but by the acceptability of the sacrifice presented for them.

This entire system, day after day, year after year, was never meant to be the final solution.
Hebrews 10:1-4 says the law and its sacrifices were a *"shadow of the good things to come"*, reminding the people of sin but never fully removing it.

That's why when John the Baptizer saw Jesus approaching, he didn't just call Him "Teacher, Rabbi," or even "Messiah."

He cried out:
"Behold the Lamb of God who takes away the sin of the world!" (John 1:29)

John recognized that the entire prophetic weight of the sacrificial system was pointing forward to this Lamb.

The perfect, unblemished, and final Lamb!

Key truth: The people's purity did not secure atonement; the lamb's purity did.

- The Old covenant sacrifices had to be repeated because they were imperfect.
- Jesus the Lamb of God, offered one perfect sacrifice, once and for all (Hebrews 10:10-14)
- Our hope, assurance, and salvation rest not in our

moral consistency, but in the unchanging perfection of the Lamb who was slain.

This breaks the chains of performance-based religion.
You are not saved because you are flawless.
You are saved because the Lamb is flawless.
You are not accepted because
you bring a perfect offering.
You are accepted because you trust in the perfect offering God provided…His Son.

Because of the Lamb:
- We are not just **forgiven**; we are **recreated**.
- We are not just **escaping judgment**;
we are **stepping into sonship**.
- We are not just **heading to heaven**;
we are **carrying heaven's nature**.

Hebrews 10:14 declares, *"For by one offering He has perfected forever those who are being sanctified."*

This means:
- The blood addresses past, present, and future.
- The blood covers not only actions but identity.
- The blood does not merely postpone judgment, it fully satisfies it.

The Lamb is central to salvation because only the Lamb's perfection could substitute for humanity's imperfection.

Salvation is **not a reward for good behavior** or a moral upgrade, it is the **total, transforming result of the Lamb's finished work**.

When we understand the Lamb's role, we stop striving for worthiness and start living from the security of what He has already accomplished.

Salvation is not:

- God ignoring judgment
- God softening the standard
- God magically shielding sinners

Salvation is:
- God satisfying justice
- God providing a substitute
- God legally declaring:

"The penalty has been fully paid"

This why Paul can write in Romans 8:1, *"There is therefore now no condemnation to those who are in Christ Jesus..."*

Not because God pretends we never sinned, but because the blood of the Lamb proclaims:

THEY SHALL BE SAVED

"The death sentence has already been carried out...in Him"

Closing Declaration:
"I am redeemed not because of my purity, but because of the Lamb's."
"I am saved not because I perform, but because the blood has spoken."
"I am made new, not because I earned it, but because the Lamb was slain."

Reflection Questions

1. What does the blood on the doorpost in Exodus 12 truly signify, and how does it shift your understanding of salvation? How does viewing the blood as a legal declaration, rather than a magical protection, change how you see the cross?

2. How is substitutionary death central to the Gospel message? In what ways have you tried to avoid or soften the truth that death was the necessary price for sin?

3. Why was it essential that the lamb be without blemish? What does this requirement teach you about the nature of Christ and the insufficiency of human effort in salvation?

4. How does the statement "It wasn't the absence of death, but the presence of substitutionary death that saved them" speak to your personal walk with God?

5. John the Baptist called Jesus "the Lamb of God who takes away the sin of the world." Why is it significant that he used the title Lamb instead of Messiah or King in that moment?

6. What does Hebrews 10:14 mean to you when it says that Jesus "has perfected forever those who are being sanctified"? How does this impact your understanding of spiritual growth and the process of sanctification?

7. Are there ways you've unknowingly lived by performance-based religion instead of resting in the finished work of the Lamb? How can you realign your faith with grace rather than effort?

8. What does it mean to you personally that "the death sentence has already been carried out… in Him"? How can this truth bring freedom from condemnation or guilt in your life?

9. How does understanding Jesus as the perfect Lamb reshape your view of worthiness and acceptance before God?

"The atonement nor our redemption was about the merits of a man, but the purity of the Lamb."

— **Christopher Turney**

Chapter 4
Identity Over Destination

For many, salvation is understood primarily as a change of destination, a way to escape hell and secure heaven. But Scripture reveals something far more powerful: salvation is about a complete **change of identity**.

The Gospel is not merely about where you will go when you die; it is about who you are right now and who you have become in Christ.

2 Corinthians 5:17 says, *"If anyone is in Christ, he is a new creation; old things have passed away; behold, all things have become new."*

The Greek term kainē ktisis means something **never seen before**, a new kind of creation, not just a cleaned-up or improved old version.

You are not simply a forgiven sinner. You are not a polished-up Adam. You are a recreated being, born of the Spirit, partaking of divine nature (2 Peter 1:4).

This is critical:
It does not simply mean we are restored to Adams original state before he fell.

Why? Because what God has accomplished in Christ goes far beyond merely fixing Adam's failure.
Adam before the fall, was innocent but untested, he had the potential to fall.
In Christ, we are righteous and secure, we are joined to One who has already overcome death and the grave.

"We are a peculiar people"

Adam was a living soul (1 Corinthians 15:45);
Christ is a life-giving Spirit.
We are not just returned to Eden; we are united with the rise, glorified Christ, something Adam never tasted.

New creatures participating in Christ's resurrection!

We are not restored to pre-fall innocence; we are raised into post-resurrection life; life that has already conquered sin, death, and the grave.

If we think we have only returned to pre-fall Adam, we might think we could "fall" again.
But in Christ, we are placed in a **completely new order**, one secured by His finished work, His indestructible life, and His eternal victory.

We are not patching up the old.
We are stepping into something entirely new, permanent, and divine.

THEY SHALL BE SAVED

New Wine, New Wineskins

Jesus said in Luke 5:37-38 (NKJV):
"And no one puts new wine into old wineskins; or else the new wine will burst the wineskins and be spilled, and the wineskins will be ruined. But new wine must be put into new wineskins, and both are preserved."

The principle here is simple but profound:

You can't fit a completely new thing into an old, inflexible structure.

The new wine of the Kingdom, the new covenant, the new life, requires a new container.

When Pul wrote of the kainē ktisis he's describing not a patched-up Adam, not a repaired humanity, but a **completely new order**.
An order capable of carrying the life, Spirit, and resurrection power of Christ.
You can't put the indwelling Spirit of God inside an old Adamic identity.
You can't mix grace and law, flesh and Spirit, old covenant and new covenant.
You need a **new wineskin**, and God provides it by making you a **new creation**.

Key truth: Salvation does not just change your status before God; it changes your essence. You are now in

Christ, joined to His life, and clothed in His righteousness.

Colossians 1:13 says, *"He has delivered us from the power of darkness and conveyed us into the kingdom of the Son of His love."*

Salvation doesn't just stamp your passport to heaven; it **transfers your citizenship**.

You now live under:
- A **new King** (Jesus)
- A **new government** (Kingdom of God)
- A **new law** (the law of the Spirit of life, Romans 8:2)
- A **new family** (Galatians 4:7)

You don't operate from earth upward trying to reach God, you operate from heaven downward, carrying the resources, authority, and mission of His Kingdom.

Romans 8:15–17 says, *"You did not receive the spirit of bondage again to fear, but you received the Spirit of adoption by whom we cry out, 'Abba, Father.' The Spirit Himself bears witness… that we are children of God, and if children, then heirs, heirs of God and joint heirs with Christ."*

Paul wanted us to understand that **salvation is not another kind of slavery**. We are not moving from slavery to sin into slavery to religious performance or fear. *"You have not received the spirit of slavery again* *to fear."* In other words: fear not, this is **not slavery**; this is **sonship**.

You were not just **saved from judgment**; you were **adopted into inheritance**.
You were not just **spared from death**; you were **positioned for dominion**.

Many Christians live as though salvation is a ticket that only activates after death. But salvation is a present possession:

- Eternal life begins the moment you believe (John 5:24).
- The Spirit of God comes to live within you now (1 Corinthians 6:19).
- You are seated with Christ in heavenly places now (Ephesians 2:6).

You are not waiting for eternal life to begin, you are living it now as you walk in your new nature.

Salvation is not just the forgiveness of past sins:
- It is the **rebirth of a new heart** (Ezekiel 36:26).
- It is the indwelling of the Holy Spirit (Romans 8:11).
- It is the exchange of Adam's inheritance for Christ's (Romans 5:19).

You are no longer defined by your past, your failures, or your family's history.

You are defined by Christ's victory, Christ's life, and Christ's love.

When you understand salvation as identity, you stop striving to be accepted and start living from acceptance. You stop performing to earn God's love and start walking in the love that was freely given.

Galatians 2:20 says, *"I have been crucified with Christ; it is no longer I who live, but Christ lives in me..."*

Biblical salvation is not about where you go when you die, it is about who you become in Christ before you die.
Salvation is not about what we are saved from but rather what are we saved to.
- We are saved to life - (John 10:10)
- We are saved to sonship - (Galatians 4:4-7)
- We are saved to inheritance – (1 Peter 1:3-4)
- We are saved to a Kingdom – (Colossians 1:13)
- We are saved to glorification – (Romans 8:30)

When we put our faith in Christ this is what we receive; not a fire insurance policy, nor a ticket to escape hell. Our part is believing in His part.

It could be said that we are saved from:
- Sin and its power
- The wrath of God
- The domain of darkness

- The curse of the law
- Death and the grave

These things we have been told we are saved from Christ defeated completely.

Conclusion:
Salvation is not about where you are going when you die, it's about who you have become in Christ right now.
It's about stepping into your identity as a child of God, living from heaven's resources, and reflecting the image of Christ on earth.

Closing Declaration:
"I am not just saved from judgment, I am adopted into sonship.
I am not just waiting for heaven, I am walking in heaven's identity now.
I am not just forgiven, I am recreated, reborn, and restored.
I live as a child of God, carrying His name, His nature, and His glory."

Reflection Questions

1. Before reading this chapter, how would you have defined salvation? Has your perspective shifted? If so, how?

2. What does it mean to you that you are a "new creation" (2 Corinthians 5:17)? In what areas of your life do you need to embrace this truth more fully?

3. How does viewing salvation as identity (rather than just destination) impact your understanding of your daily walk with Christ?

4. The chapter says we are not restored to Adam's innocence but raised into Christ's victory. What is the difference between the two, and why does it matter?

5. Jesus spoke of "new wine needing new wineskins." In what ways have you tried to fit the new life of the Spirit into old patterns or mindsets?

6. What does it mean to live from heaven downward rather than from earth upward? How does this shape your decisions, prayers, and relationships?

7. Romans 8:15–17 speaks of adoption, not fear. Do you still carry any fear-based mindset in your relationship with God? What would it look like to fully walk in the Spirit of adoption?

8. Which of the "saved to" truths most resonates with you: life, sonship, inheritance, the Kingdom, or glorification? Why?

9. In your own words, how would you now explain to someone that salvation is about who you become, not just where you go?

10. Read Galatians 2:20. How does this verse challenge or affirm the way you currently live your life in Christ?

Chapter 5
Kingdom Salvation

Salvation is often presented in narrow, individual terms: "One person repents." "One soul is saved." But when Jesus preached the Gospel of the Kingdom, He offered a vision far bigger than just individual escape from judgment, He pointed to household redemption, community transformation, and cultural reformation.

"God does not save individuals in isolation. He saves families, generations, and nations through covenant." – Anonymous

Salvation in the Kingdom touches more than hearts; it touches houses, economies, systems, and nations.

In Luke 19, Zacchaeus, the chief tax collector, climbed a tree to see Jesus. He was rich, aligned with the Roman system, and despised by his own people. When Jesus called him down, Zacchaeus did more than express personal faith, he made a public, economic, and social break from his corrupt alliances:
- He offered to restore what he had stolen.
- He vowed to repay those he had defrauded fourfold.
- He repositioned his household from Roman oppression into Kingdom alignment.

And Jesus declared, "Today salvation has come to this house…" (Luke 19:9). Notice: Jesus didn't say, "Zacchaeus, you are saved." He said, "Salvation has come to this house."

Kingdom salvation brings a household shift, it reorders the values, priorities, and spiritual covering over an entire family.

"Noah didn't build the ark just for himself. God's salvation plan always included a household." – Dutch Sheets

Throughout Scripture, God's redemptive acts often involved whole households:
- Noah and his family were saved through the ark (Genesis 7:1).
- Rahab and her household were spared from Jericho's destruction (Joshua 2:12–13).
- Cornelius' whole house received the Holy Spirit (Acts 10:44–48).
- The Philippian jailer's entire household was baptized (Acts 16:31–34).

Salvation in the Kingdom is not isolated; it is generational.

"The Kingdom doesn't just save souls, it reclaims territories." – Dr. Myles Munroe

Kingdom salvation is also territorial. When Jesus delivered the Gadarene demoniac (Mark 5), He didn't just liberate one man, He reclaimed an entire region from demonic control. The man who was once chained and isolated became a preacher of the gospel in Decapolis. In one act, a life was changed, but so was a city's atmosphere. The King doesn't just rescue people; He reclaims territory.

The Gospel is not only about personal deliverance; it's about the transfer of entire realms:
- Economies shift when Kingdom justice takes root (Proverbs 11:10).
- Communities heal when Kingdom mercy flows (Micah 6:8).
- Nations change when Kingdom righteousness is established (Isaiah 60:1–3).

When salvation is rightly understood through the lens of the Kingdom, it becomes clear that it cannot be contained within private piety or personal devotion alone. It was never meant to be hidden in a corner. Like leaven in dough, Kingdom salvation permeates every level of society. It starts in the heart but doesn't stop until it manifests in houses, neighborhoods, industries, and institutions.

Religion often shrinks salvation to "souls for heaven," but Jesus' Gospel was about heaven's reign on earth (Matthew 6:10).

Key truth: Kingdom salvation does not just pull people out of sin; it establishes the King's government over every sphere they touch. Religion tends to measure success one convert at a time. But the Gospel of the Kingdom expands the vision:
- Families reconciled
- Generational curses broken
- Systems reformed
- Cultures renewed

Colossians 1:13 says, *"He has delivered us from the power of darkness and conveyed us into the kingdom of the Son of His love."* This transfer is not just individual, it ripples outward into everything connected to the believer.

This is why a believer's home should feel different. Why a Spirit-filled business should operate with different ethics. Why Kingdom people should raise children with generational vision, not survival instincts. Because wherever the King reigns, His culture invades.

When you understand Kingdom salvation,
you stop thinking small:
- You stop praying only for your own needs
and start praying for your family line.
- You stop limiting God's work to your heart
and start inviting Him into your workplace,
your community, your city.

THEY SHALL BE SAVED

- You stop believing salvation is just about "escaping hell" and start living as an agent of heaven's invasion.

Kingdom salvation is contagious. It multiplies influence, establishes covenant patterns, and creates cultures where righteousness can flourish. It doesn't stop at your front door. It knocks on the doors of institutions, schools, governments, and nations with the message: "The King has come."

Conclusion:
Kingdom salvation means your life, your family, your business, your neighborhood, and your culture come under the reign of the King. It is not just about getting people out of hell; it is about bringing heaven's order into earth's broken systems.

Closing Declaration:
"Salvation has come to my house.
Salvation has come to my family.
Salvation has come to my work and my city.
I am not just saved alone; I carry Kingdom transformation wherever I go."

Reflection Questions

1. What stood out to you about Jesus' words to Zacchaeus, "Today salvation has come to this house"? How does this challenge or expand your understanding of salvation?

2. Can you identify areas in your life where salvation has not just changed your heart, but also your household, work, or community? What evidence of transformation can you trace to the reign of Christ in those areas?

3. In what ways have you seen or experienced salvation as generational rather than just personal? Are you praying and believing for household or family salvation? Why is that important?

4. How does the concept of Kingdom salvation shift your focus from individual escape to cultural transformation? What are some practical ways you can carry the Kingdom into systems or environments you're part of?

5. Do you see yourself as a carrier of Kingdom transformation, or have you limited salvation to "going to heaven"? What changes when you begin to live as an agent of heaven's invasion?

6. Think of the institutions or territories you're connected to (school, city, workplace, etc.). What might it look like for "salvation to come to that house" through your presence?

7. How do you interpret Colossians 1:13 in the context of your daily life? What does it mean for you to live as someone who has been conveyed into the Kingdom of the Son?

8. Is there a system, family line, or region you feel called to influence with Kingdom values? How might you begin praying and acting toward reformation in that area?

Chapter 6
The Power and Permanence of Redemption

A common and deeply debated question among believers is: If a person is truly saved, can they lose their salvation? If we didn't gain salvation by works, can we lose it by works? And if God calls it "eternal life," how can it be temporary?

Ephesians 2:8–9 reminds us, "For by grace you have been saved through faith, and that not of yourselves; it is the gift of God, not of works…"

John 1:12–13 says, "But as many as received Him, to them He gave the right to become children of God… who were born, not of blood, nor of the will of the flesh, nor of the will of man, but of God."

Jesus reinforces this in John 6:44: "No one can come to Me unless the Father who sent Me draws him…" And Paul echoes it in 1 Corinthians 12:3: "…no one can say that Jesus is Lord except by the Holy Spirit."

Salvation is initiated by God, secured by God, and preserved by God. Jesus declared in John 10:28–29,

"I give them eternal life, and they shall never perish; neither shall anyone snatch them out of My hand." We are not holding onto God, He is holding onto us.

This truth provides an anchor for the soul in turbulent times. When doubts arise, or when failures make us question our worth, the permanence of redemption reminds us that our security is not rooted in our feelings, but in God's faithfulness. *"When I cannot hold Him, He still holds me,"* wrote Charles Spurgeon. That is the essence of grace.

Hebrews 10:14 says, "For by one offering He has perfected forever those who are being sanctified." This means:
- The blood of Jesus covers past, present, and future.
- The blood redeems not only actions but identity.
- The blood does not need constant reapplication, it speaks once, for all time.

1 John 2:19 says, "They went out from us, but they were not of us; for if they had been of us, they would have continued with us." True salvation results in a transformed life and enduring faith. Works do not secure salvation, but they evidence it. Perseverance is not the cause of salvation, it is the fruit.

Ephesians 1:13–14 says we are "sealed with the Holy Spirit of promise, who is the guarantee of our inheritance…" This seal is not fragile or weak, it is God's mark of ownership.

You didn't save yourself, and you don't sustain yourself. Salvation is God's work from beginning to end.

Jesus says in John 5:24, "He who hears My word and believes in Him who sent Me has everlasting life, and shall not come into judgment, but has passed from death into life." We don't wait for eternal life to begin when we die; we possess it now, and by definition, it cannot end.

As A.W. Tozer once said, *"We are saved to be saved. Salvation is not a one-time transaction, but a continuing, transforming possession."* Eternal life is not fragile or subject to expiration, it is the unshakeable evidence of union with Christ.

A person cannot truly have eternal life and then lose it, because eternal life is God's unbreakable, irrevocable gift. It is secured not by human effort but by Christ's finished work.

The real question is not, can you lose salvation?

but, Have you truly been born again to possess it?

As Martin Luther boldly declared, *"Our salvation does not depend on our own strength, but on the promise of*

God, which cannot fail." And as Corrie ten Boom reminded us, *"There is no pit so deep that God's love is not deeper still."*

Closing Declaration:
"I am not holding on to eternal life, eternal life is holding on to me.
I am not kept by my works, I am kept by God's promise.
I am not wondering if I'm secure, I am anchored in Christ forever."

Reflection Questions

1. How does understanding salvation as a gift from God, not earned by works, change the way you relate to God? Read Ephesians 2:8–9. Do you still find yourself trying to earn His approval?

2. What does it mean to you that eternal life begins now and not just after death? How might this truth reshape your view of daily Christian living?

3. In what ways have you been tempted to think your salvation depends on your own performance? How does John 10:28–29 confront or correct that thinking?

4. What comfort or assurance do you find in the idea that God is the One who draws, saves, and seals? Consider how that impacts your confidence during times of failure or doubt.

5. Hebrews 10:14 says we have been "perfected forever." What does that mean to you personally? Does this truth lead you toward greater freedom or responsibility? Why?

6. Can you identify areas where you confuse spiritual fruit with spiritual root? Are you measuring your salvation by your works rather than letting works be the evidence of your salvation?

7. Do you believe your salvation is secure? Why or why not? How do Scriptures like Romans 8:38–39 and John 5:24 influence your answer?

8. How would you respond to someone who says, "If salvation is permanent, won't people just live however they want?" What role does transformation and the fruit of the Spirit play in this conversation?

Chapter 7
Restored to Our Origin

From the very beginning, there have only been two kinds of humanity: Those in Adam, and those in Christ. This is not just a theological category, it is a truth that shapes your very existence, your identity, and your destiny.

Ephesians 1:3–5 tells us: *"Blessed be the God and Father of our Lord Jesus Christ, who has blessed us with every spiritual blessing in the heavenly places in Christ, just as He chose us in Him before the foundation of the world..."*

You were not merely created by your earthly parents, you were known by God before time began. You came through your parents, but you came from God.

Before your body was formed, your existence was held in Christ. You were part of God's eternal plan, carved out of His heart, created in Christ before the foundation of the world.

God says to Jeremiah in Jeremiah 1:5: *"Before I formed you in the womb I knew you; before you were born I sanctified you; I ordained you..."*

This reveals a staggering truth: We existed in the mind and purpose of God before we had physical form. We were not just known; we were blessed, eulogized, by the Father.

In Ephesians 1:3, Paul writes: *"Blessed be the God and Father of our Lord Jesus Christ, who has blessed us with every spiritual blessing in the heavenly places in Christ..."*

The Greek word here is eulogéō, it means to speak well of, to pronounce good over, to praise or celebrate with words. It's where we get the word eulogy, a speech that speaks honor and goodness over someone's life.

Here's the revelation: We were not eulogized after we died; we were eulogized before we were born!

Before you ever failed, God spoke His blessing over you. Before you ever sinned, God pronounced good over you. Before you were ever shaped in the womb, God declared who you were and what you were destined for in Christ.

Redemption is not God scrambling to fix what went wrong. It is God restoring us to our original identity, the "in whom" we were created.

2 Corinthians 5:17 says: *"If anyone is in Christ, he is a new creation..."* This is not merely a patch on Adam's failure, it is a re-creation of God's eternal design: sons

and daughters reflecting His image, walking in His authority, and sharing His life.

John writes in 1 John 2:20–21: "But you have an anointing from the Holy One, and you know all things… I have not written to you because you do not know the truth, but because you know it…"

Revelation is not the discovery of something new; it is the remembrance of what God spoke from the beginning.

When we receive revelation, it is as though the veil is lifted, and we remember ancient truths planted in us from before time. The word "apocalypse" means uncovering, it's not adding something new; it's unveiling what was always there.

John says in his Gospel (John 1:1–4) that in the beginning was the Word, and through the Word all things were made. When God said, *"Let there be light,"* (Genesis 1:3), we were there in Christ, hidden, represented, and destined.

Salvation is the return, the homecoming, the restoration to the One in whom we were created originally. It is not just being saved from something bad; it is being restored to something eternal.

Christopher K. Turney

We Were Created in the Image — That Image Is Christ

Genesis 1:27 tells us we were made in the image of God. But Colossians 1:15 clarifies that Christ is the image of the invisible God. That means we weren't just made like Him; we were made in Him.

This is profound: to be in Christ now is not an upgrade from Adam, it is a return to the One in whom we were created before time began. When Paul writes, *"If any man be in Christ, he is a new creation,"* he is revealing that we are being repositioned into our original blueprint. The "new creation" is actually the ancient design, restored, not replaced.

We are not merely forgiven sinners given a second chance. We are recreated beings, those who now live out of our creation (in Christ), not our formation (in Adam). This is not just as though we didn't sin, it is as if Adam never sinned, because we are now found in the Last Adam, Christ, who has conquered death and reversed the curse.

That means we weren't just made to resemble a distant deity; we were created in Christ Himself. He is not merely a reflection of God's nature; He is the substance from which we were drawn. So, it's not speaking of something entirely new in time, it's the restoration of something original in eternity. To be in Christ is to return to the One we were originally designed in before the foundation of the world.

Formation vs. Creation: What's the Difference?

- Formation is your earthly beginning, your physical body, shaped in time and space.

- Creation is your eternal origin, your spiritual identity, created in Christ before the world began.

Genesis 2:7 shows that Adam was formed from the dust. But Ephesians 2:10 reveals that we are created in Christ Jesus for good works. The first man was of the earth; the second Man is the Lord from heaven (1 Corinthians 15:47).

When you are born again, you don't just receive a new behavior, you recover your eternal blueprint. You are not living from your formation; you are restored to your creation in Christ.

Your formation, the body formed from dust, is your earth suit. But your creation, your essence, is divine. You were created in Christ before time began, and salvation repositions you back into that eternal blueprint. You are no longer in the lineage of the first Adam, bound by sin and shame; you have been transferred into the last Adam, Christ Himself, where your true origin is restored.

Now, you can live from your creation, not your formation, from your divine identity, not your earthly history. This is not self-improvement; it is sonship remembered. Not becoming something else, but being placed back in the One you were always in.

And here is the deeper mystery:

To be *"in Christ"* is to be restored to our eternal design, not simply innocence, but incorruptible life. It is not just that we are saved from sin; we are placed back into the place of origin, a place untouched by the fall.

This is not merely as though we didn't sin. It is as though Adam never did.

In Christ, we are not living from the residue of failure, we are living from the root of eternal purpose.

This is why Paul writes that we are *"created in Christ Jesus for good works, which God prepared beforehand"* (Ephesians 2:10).

Not just forgiven… but recreated in the very image of the eternal Son.

Not just reset… but reinstated in a realm that existed before time. a realm of unbreakable union with God.

Jesus did not come to make us better versions of fallen man; He came to reveal a new man, one born from above, not of the will of flesh, nor of man, but of God (John 1:13).

This is eternal life, not just duration, but dimension. Not just living forever, but living from an uncreated, indestructible place.

To be in Christ is to be in the One who has no beginning and no end.

And salvation is not merely a future reward, it is a present reality, the restoration of who we were always meant to be before Adam ever fell.

When you understand salvation this way:
- You stop striving to earn belonging.
- You stop thinking of redemption as an afterthought.
- You start living as one who is remembering who you were always meant to be.

Revelation is not simply learning; it is recovering the memory of your divine origin, your Father's voice, and your eternal destiny.

Conclusion:
To be redeemed is to be restored to your true origin, to remember that you were created in Christ, blessed in Christ, known in Christ, and now recreated in Christ.

Salvation does not make you someone else; it makes you fully who you were always meant to be.

Closing Declaration:

"I was not just created on earth, I was known in heaven.
I did not come from my parents, I came through them, from God.
I am not just learning truth, I am remembering truth.
I am not just saved, I am restored to my eternal origin in Christ."

Reflection Questions

1. What does it mean to you personally that you were "known in Christ before the foundation of the world"? How does this affect how you view yourself, past, present, and future?

2. How does the idea of being "created in Christ" differ from being merely formed in the womb? Which truth feels more permanent to you, and why?

3. In what ways have you lived more out of your "formation" than your "creation"? What practical shifts can you make to begin living from your original identity?

4. If salvation is a restoration to your origin, what are you being restored from, and what are you being restored to? Consider areas in your life where you've believed you were just "patched up" rather than made new.

5. What does it mean to be repositioned in Christ instead of remaining in Adam? How does this shift your understanding of identity, inheritance, and authority?

6. Why is it significant that Christ is the "image" in whom we were created? (Colossians 1:15–17) How does this shape your understanding of being made in God's image?

7. What "truths" about your life do you feel the Holy Spirit is helping you remember rather than learn for the first time? Reflect on moments where it felt like something in your spirit "woke up" to who you were all along.

8. In what ways do you see redemption as more than forgiveness, but as a recovery of divine intention? How can this deeper view of redemption impact your worship, purpose, and relationships?

Chapter 8
Living as the Redeemed

Salvation is not the end of the story, it's the beginning of a new life. Being redeemed is not just about being saved from something (sin, death, separation); it's about being saved into something: a life of sonship, purpose, authority, and fellowship with God.

2 Corinthians 5:17 reminds us: "If anyone is in Christ, he is a new creation; old things have passed away; behold, all things have become new."

We no longer live under:
- Old labels
- Old failures
- Old limitations

We live from a new identity:
- I am a child of God (John 1:12)
- I am a citizen of heaven (Philippians 3:20)
- I am the righteousness of God in Christ (2 Corinthians 5:21)
- I am an heir of God and joint heir with Christ (Romans 8:17)

Redemption rewrites our reference point. The cross becomes the dividing line between who we were and who we now are. We do not live trying to make up for the past, we live anchored in the truth that Jesus settled the past and authored our future. Our lives are no longer defined by sin's residue but by redemption's reality.

Living as the redeemed means living from who you are, not just from what you do.

Romans 8:37 says, "In all these things we are more than conquerors through Him who loved us." We are not meant to live in fear, defeat, or striving. We live from Christ's victory, not toward it.

When you live from the position of redemption, every day becomes a declaration: I am no longer bound by guilt, shame, or spiritual insecurity. My past is not my platform, Christ is. You are not climbing to be accepted, you are standing because you are already chosen, already seated, already secure.

Key aspects of redeemed living:
- Standing in grace, not striving for approval (Romans 5:1–2)
- Walking in the Spirit, not fulfilling the flesh (Galatians 5:16)
- Exercising Kingdom authority on earth (Luke 10:19)

THEY SHALL BE SAVED

To live redeemed is to live reconciled.

2 Corinthians 5:18–20 tells us we have been given the ministry of reconciliation. We are not just recipients of grace, we are carriers of it. We live as ambassadors, representing the Kingdom in:
- Our families
- Our workplaces
- Our communities
- The nations

Redemption is more than a personal gift; it's a public commission. Redeemed people become bridges, reconciling others to God, redeeming moments for eternity, and revealing a Kingdom not of this world.

Redeemed people live on mission, reflecting the heart and reign of their King.

Galatians 4:7 says, "Therefore you are no longer a slave but a son, and if a son, then an heir of God through Christ."

We don't live striving for God's approval or fearing His rejection. We live as sons and daughters, confident, loved, and entrusted with Kingdom purpose.

The redeemed life is not passive; it's powerful. It is rooted in the finished work of Christ, but it bears fruit in everyday life. Redeemed people speak differently, love differently, work differently, and lead differently because they carry heaven's influence on earth.

Conclusion:
Living as the redeemed is not about trying harder; it's about walking in the new nature God has already given. It's about resting in Christ's finished work and carrying His life into every area of the world.

Closing Declaration:
"I live as the redeemed.
I walk in sonship, not slavery.
I carry heaven's authority, not earth's limitations.
I am not just saved, I am sent.
I am not just healed, I am commissioned.
I am the redeemed of the Lord, and I say so!"

Reflection Questions

1. What does being "redeemed" mean to you personally, beyond just being forgiven? How has your understanding of redemption shifted through this chapter?

2. In what areas of your life are you still tempted to live from your past instead of your new identity in Christ? What truths from this chapter can help you overcome those areas?

3. Which new identity declaration (e.g., child of God, righteousness of God, joint heir with Christ) do you struggle to fully embrace, and why?

4. Are you living from Christ's victory, or striving toward it? How does Romans 8:37 challenge your current mindset?

5. How are you exercising your Kingdom authority in daily life? What would it look like for you to walk more boldly in Luke 10:19?

6. In what ways are you carrying the ministry of reconciliation in your relationships, work, or community? Is there a specific place or person God is calling you to be an ambassador of His Kingdom?

7. How does the truth that you are a son or daughter (not a slave) affect how you pray, serve, and lead? What does Galatians 4:7 stir in your spirit?

8. Are you living with a sense of Kingdom mission, or just personal survival? How can you transition from being just "saved" to being "sent" as a redeemed representative?

9. What does redeemed living look like in your workplace, home, or local community? Are there areas where heaven's culture still needs to be carried in through your influence?

10. What part of the closing declaration resonates most deeply with you right now? Write it down, meditate on it, and begin declaring it daily.

Chapter 9
The Adam Exchange

Many believers understand salvation as Jesus dying for their sins. While true, that statement only scratches the surface.

The real power of the gospel is not just that Christ died for what you've done, but that He came to undo what you were born under.

You were not just rescued from personal mistakes; you were delivered from an inherited, universal Adamic condition, a human legacy of corruption, death, and separation from God that began long before you were born.

Romans 5:12 says: "Therefore, just as through one man sin entered the world, and death through sin, and thus death spread to all men, because all sinned…"

It was through one man that sin and death entered. Death did not wait for each individual to personally sin, it spread because of Adam's action.

Adam's rebellion unleashed not just guilt, but a universal condition: corruption, mortality, separation, futility, a world system governed by decay.

John 1:14 tells us: *"And the Word became flesh and dwelt among us..."* But whose flesh? It wasn't pristine, untainted, pre-fall human flesh. It was the post-fall humanity of Adam's descendants.

Christ put on Adam's condition, not Adam's guilt (for He was sinless), but Adam's vulnerability, mortality, and exposure to death.

You cannot redeem what you do not fully enter. You cannot destroy what you refuse to touch.

Galatians 3:27: *"For as many of you as were baptized into Christ have put on Christ."*

You are now clothed in Christ, because He first clothed Himself in Adam.

He took on our Adamic condition, so we could take on His resurrected identity. He absorbed Adam's curse, so we could walk in Christ's blessing. He wore Adam's death, so we could wear Christ's life.

This is the power of reconciliation. The Greek word for *"reconciliation"* in 2 Corinthians 5:18 is katallagē, meaning a mutual exchange. It's not simply an apology accepted, or peace restored, it is the surrender of one thing in order to receive something entirely different.

Christ did not just forgive our sins; He exchanged our death for His life. And this wasn't a transaction that started 2,000 years ago, it was a journey back to the root of our fall. He reached all the way back to the garden where death began. He didn't merely cancel the curse; He reversed the condition. He gave His eternal life in place of Adam's inherited death. This is the true depth of redemption: Jesus didn't just receive your repentance; He took your death and gave you His resurrection.

Throughout His ministry, Jesus addressed God intimately as Abba, except for one chilling moment. On the cross, He cried: *"Eloi, Eloi, lama sabachthani?" "My God, My God, why have You forsaken Me?"*

Why the shift? Because at that moment, He wasn't standing as the Son addressing His Father; He was standing as Adam, addressing Elohim, the Creator, the Lawgiver.

On the cross, He was carrying the collective death humanity had inherited, crying out under Adam's broken covenant.

This moment was profound. Jesus, who always said *"Father,"* now says *"Eloi",* invoking the name of the Creator (Elohim), the One who breathed into Adam, the One who said, *"In the day you eat of it, you shall surely die."*

He was not just speaking to His Father in heaven, He was addressing the God of Genesis, the Lawgiver of Eden, the One who first confronted death's consequence. Jesus' cry was not just about Calvary; it was about Eden.

On the cross, He walked back through time and presented Himself to the first Adam. He said in effect, *"I will take your death and offer you, My life."* This was not simply forgiveness at the scene of the crime, it was restoration at the scene of the fall. Jesus redeemed humanity not just forward from the cross but backward to the garden.

This mutual exchange was not limited to Calvary.

Christ had been moving through history long before the cross, appearing again and again:

- Abraham met Him as Melchizedek.
- Joshua encountered Him as the Commander of the Lord's army.
- Isaiah saw Him exalted.
- Nebuchadnezzar witnessed Him as the fourth man in the fire.

In each of these moments, Christ was reaching back, prefiguring the cross, intervening long before they knew His name.

THEY SHALL BE SAVED

Romans 5:19 says: *"For as by one man's disobedience many were made sinners, so also by one Man's obedience many will be made righteous."*

Christ came not just to cover Adam's legacy, but to destroy it.

1 John 3:8: *"For this purpose the Son of God was manifested, that He might destroy the works of the devil."*

The cross was not just a payment; it was an execution of Adam's entire fallen line.

Here's what this means for you:
You are not just forgiven, you are made new.
You are not just released from guilt,
you are released from condemnation.
You are not just a better version of yourself,
you are a new creation.

2 Corinthians 5:17: *"Therefore, if anyone is in Christ, he is a new creation; old things have passed away; behold, all things have become new."*

You no longer live as a son of Adam. You live as a son of God.

When Jesus cried, "Why have You spared Me?", He was absorbing the unbearable weight of Adam's death, so that you and I could be raised as sons.

You are not called to live under Adam's shadow. You are called to walk in Christ's light.

This is the Adam exchange: He wore your death so you could wear His life. He stepped into Adam so you could step into Christ.

Romans 8:1–2 says: *"There is therefore now no condemnation to those who are in Christ Jesus... For the law of the Spirit of life in Christ Jesus has made me free from the law of sin and death."*

Reflection Questions

1. What does it mean to you that Jesus did not just die for your sins but reversed the condition you were born under in Adam? How does this change the way you view your salvation?

2. How does the biblical definition of reconciliation (katallagē – mutual exchange) challenge the common phrase "I gave my life to Jesus"? What did you actually "give," and what did He truly give you?

3. Why is it significant that Jesus called out "Eloi" on the cross instead of "Father"? How does this reveal His redemptive mission reaching back to Eden?

4. How does understanding that you were "in Adam" help you appreciate what it means to now be "in Christ"? What are the implications of no longer living as a descendant of Adam but as a son of God?

5. In what ways are you still tempted to live under Adam's shadow (guilt, striving, separation)? How can you begin walking fully in the light and life of Christ today?

6. Jesus became what you were so you could become what He is. How does this truth empower your identity, confidence, and calling?

7. If the cross was not just payment but the execution of Adam's line, how should that affect your relationship with your past? What does it mean for your future?

Chapter 10
Saved by Grace

Salvation is one of the most breathtaking and humbling truths of Scripture, not because of what we do, but because of what God has done. From beginning to end, salvation is a gift of grace, not a product of human effort, achievement, or merit.

Ephesians 2:8–9 proclaims: *"For by grace you have been saved through faith, and that not of yourselves; it is the gift of God, not of works, lest anyone should boast."*

This truth anchors us. We are not saved by climbing a spiritual ladder, cleaning up our act, or earning divine favor. We are saved because God, in His mercy, reached down to rescue us.

Not by Works

Titus 3:5 says, *"Not by works of righteousness which we have done, but according to His mercy He saved us…"*

Our best efforts, even the good, noble, religious ones, cannot secure salvation. Works can never tip the scale because the standard is perfection, and only Christ meets it.

Isaiah 64:6 reminds us that *"all our righteousnesses are like filthy rags."* Salvation is not achieved; it is received.

"Grace is not a reward for the righteous; it is a gift for the guilty." — Matt Chandler

Not by Law

Romans 3:20 declares, *"By the deeds of the law no flesh will be justified in His sight, for by the law is the knowledge of sin."*

The law serves as a mirror, reflecting our flaws and pointing us to our need. It was never designed to be a ladder we climb to reach God.

Galatians 2:16 adds, *"Knowing that a man is not justified by the works of the law but by faith in Jesus Christ..."*

We are not saved by law-keeping but by trusting the One who fulfilled the law perfectly.

Not by Human Will or Lineage

John 1:12–13 says, *"But as many as received Him, to them He gave the right to become children of God...*

who were born, not of blood, nor of the will of the flesh, nor of the will of man, but of God."

Salvation is not a matter of human lineage, effort, or decision alone. It is a supernatural work, birthed by God Himself.

We are not born into the Kingdom by natural descent or human striving; we are born of God.

Grace Through Faith

While we are saved by grace, faith plays a vital role, it is the receiving hand, not the achieving hand.

Faith responds to God's initiative. It does not create salvation; it receives it. Romans 4:16 says, *"Therefore it is of faith that it might be according to grace..."*

We do not boast in our faith, for even faith itself is a gift (Ephesians 2:8).

"Faith adds nothing to grace, it simply receives it." — Watchman Nee

Grace does not just rescue us from sin; it repositions us in Christ. We were dead in trespasses, and grace made us alive together with Christ (Ephesians 2:5). This resurrection was not partial, it was complete. We are not limping toward heaven trying to earn God's smile, we are seated with Christ in heavenly places (Ephesians 2:6), the full recipients of divine favor.

Salvation by grace means that no one is beyond hope, and no one has earned a claim. The same grace that saved the thief on the cross is the grace that saves the preacher in the pulpit. This removes pride and fuels worship.

Why This Matters

When we understand that salvation is by grace:
- We live from gratitude, not performance.
- We rest in Christ's finished work,
not our unfinished efforts.
- We are free from condemnation,
knowing the law cannot save us.
- We walk humbly, knowing we did not
choose Him first, He chose us (John 15:16).

Salvation by grace magnifies God's glory
and secures our hearts in His love.

Closing Declaration:

"I am saved by grace, not by works.
I am kept by mercy, not by performance.
I am sustained by God's promise, not by my strength.
I rest, I trust, I live, in the finished work of Christ."

Reflection Questions

1. How does understanding that salvation is a gift of grace—not earned by works—affect the way you see yourself and others? Do you ever find yourself trying to earn God's approval, even after being saved?

2. What are some "works of righteousness" you've relied on in the past to feel accepted by God? How can you release those to embrace Christ's finished work?

3. Why do you think it's hard for people to accept grace without trying to add to it? In what ways do you see that tension in your own life?

4. Reflect on Titus 3:5 and Isaiah 64:6. How do these verses challenge common ideas about self-improvement and spiritual performance?

5. What's the difference between obeying God from a place of love versus a place of fear or duty? How can grace reshape your motives for obedience?

6. Why is it important to understand that even your faith is a gift (Ephesians 2:8). How does that truth protect your heart from pride or despair?

7. John 1:13 says we were born "not of blood, nor of the will of the flesh, nor of the will of man, but of God. What does it mean to you that your salvation originated in God's will, not your own effort?

8. How does the grace of God free you to live joyfully, securely, and humbly in your daily walk with Christ?

9. Think of a time when you tried to earn what God had already given. What did you learn from that experience? How can you respond differently now, knowing that you are saved by grace?

10. In what ways can you extend grace to others the way God has extended grace to you? Is there someone in your life who needs to be shown unmerited kindness?

"You contribute nothing to your salvation except the sin that made it necessary"

— Jonathan Edwards

Chapter 11
Baptized into Christ

For many believers, baptism is synonymous with water, a ceremonial act that follows a conversion experience. But Scripture presents a deeper, more eternal baptism, one not into water, but into Christ Himself. This chapter explores what it means to be baptized into Christ and how Spirit baptism, not water, is central to the New Covenant reality of salvation.

John' baptism: A prophetic precursor

John the Baptist was a voice crying out in the wilderness, preparing the way for the Messiah. His baptism was one of repentance (Matthew 3:11), urging Israel to turn from sin and ready themselves for the coming King.

But even John knew that his baptism was not the end, it was a shadow of what Jesus would bring:

"I indeed baptize you with water unto repentance, but He who is coming after me... will baptize you with the Holy Spirit and fire." (Matthew 3:11)

John's water baptism pointed to a greater baptism, one not of symbolic cleansing, but of spiritual immersion into the very life of God.

The fulfillment: baptized with the Spirit and fire

Jesus' baptism was not merely into water, but into fulfillment. When He stood in the Jordan River, He was stepping into the place of humanity, not because He needed repentance, but because He was becoming the Ark for all of those who would believe on Him.

Jesus would later baptize His people with the Holy Spirit and fire, as fulfilled on the day of Pentecost (Acts 2). That was the New Covenant baptism: not into water, but into and by the Holy Spirit.

Immersion the true meaning of baptism

The word "baptize" comes from the Greek 'baptizo', which means *"to immerse, submerge, or overwhelm."*

To be baptized *"into Christ"* (Romans 6:3) is to be immersed in His death, buried with Him, and raised with Him. It is not merely symbolic; it is spiritual participation in the finished work of Christ Jesus.

- Romans 6:3–4 Baptized into His death and raised to walk in newness of life.

- Galatians 3:27 — *"For as many of you as were baptized into Christ have put on Christ."*

Not in the name only, but in the person

Jesus commanded baptism *"in the name of the Father, Son, and Holy Spirit"* (Matthew 28:19). But this was never about a formula to be recited, it was a statement of immersion into divine identity and authority.

To be baptized *"in the name"* means to be immersed into the essence, the reality, and the full expression of that name. It means being placed under the rule, relationship, and reality of the Triune God.

Water baptism: symbolic, not salvific

While water baptism can be meaningful, it is not a prerequisite for salvation. Nowhere in the epistles do we find water baptism being preached as a condition of new birth. The thief on the cross was not baptized, yet he was promised Paradise by Jesus on the cross.

Romans 10:9–10 says salvation comes by believing in the heart and confessing with the mouth, not by entering water.

This does not diminish the meaningfulness of water baptism, but it places it in its proper context: a public declaration, but an act of symbolism not a spiritual requirement.

The true baptism that saves

The baptism that saves is the one Christ performs: immersion into His Body, His Spirit, and His life.

- 1 Corinthians 12:13 — *"For by one Spirit we were all baptized (immersed – baptidzo) into one body."*

- Titus 3:5 — *"He saved us... by the washing of regeneration and renewing of the Holy Spirit."*

- Ephesians 4:5 — *"One Lord, one faith, one baptism."*

The New Covenant baptism is Spirit-wrought, not water-based. It places us in Christ, not just in a pool.

John's baptism was not the door into the New Covenant, it was the porch. It called people to repentance in anticipation of a greater baptism to come. His ministry prepared the way for the One who would bring the New Covenant, not merely prophetically and futuristically point to it.

John himself said, *"He must increase, but I must decrease"* (John 3:30). His water baptism was transitional, a prophetic act signaling the need for cleansing, but unable to accomplish transformation. The true entrance into the New Covenant came through

Jesus, the Lamb, the Ark, the Baptizer with the Holy Spirit and fire, the King of Kings, Lord of Lords.

Jesus didn't just add to John's message; He fulfilled it. The law and the prophets **were until** John (Luke 16:16), but grace and truth came through Jesus Christ (John 1:17). That is why the baptism Jesus offers is not symbolic water, but Spirit and power, the true entrance into the Kingdom.

The law and the prophets pointed toward Christ, and His righteousness, which was fulfilled in the baptism of John. The transition is seen in that Jesus went under the water of repentance on behalf of mankind and then called us, not to a river, but to a change of mind. (Matthew 4:17).

One Faith, One Baptism:

Ephesians 4:5 says there is 'one Lord, one faith, one baptism.' This reveals that the baptism that truly unites us in the New Covenant is not the ritual of water, but the spiritual baptism into Christ. This is the covenantal immersion into the Spirit, the baptism that brings new birth, new citizenship, and new identity.

Christ, Our Ark:

Jesus did not merely go into the Jordan for a symbolic act; He went in as our Ark. Just as Noah's ark passed through judgment waters and rested on Mount Ararat, so Jesus entered the waters of John's baptism, fulfilling all righteousness.

When He came up out of the water, the heavens opened, and the Spirit descended, signaling the beginning of a New Covenant instituted by Christ Jesus.

If I am in Christ, then I was in Him when He was baptized. I was in the Ark. The righteousness He fulfilled is now fulfilled in me. I do not need to repeat the act externally to qualify, I am joined with Him spiritually, and what He fulfilled, I now walk in it. He did not merely set an example; He secured the reality.

His death satisfies God's justice and fills His wrath, and His resurrection secures my life.
His baptism becomes mine.
His obedience is credited to me.

To require water baptism for salvation is to unknowingly say, *"His obedience wasn't enough, mine must be added."*

So, if I'm in Christ:
- I reign in Him
- I ascended in Him.
- I rose in Him.
- I was buried in Him.
- I died in Him.

We have been united with Him in death so that we might be raised with Him in newness of life.

Romans 6:3–4 tells us we were baptized into His death, not a ritual bath, but a spiritual burial.

Just as I don't need to be crucified on a physical cross because He died in my place, I don't need to step into water to complete righteousness. Jesus entered the waters of baptism, the judgment, and the death, as me, for me, and with me.

He said, *"It is finished."* (John 19:30)

He didn't say, *"It is mostly finished."*

If I must be baptized in water to be saved, then I must also die to pay for my sin. But Jesus didn't leave anything undone.

Christ Fulfilled What I Could Not

And if I must fulfill any additional act, whether it be circumcision, sacrifice, or baptism, to seal my covenant status, then I would also have to suffer the penalty of sin myself.

If water baptism is required to complete my salvation, then Christ's death was insufficient.

IT IS FINISHED - NO ADDITIONS NEEDED

Reflection Questions

1. How has your understanding of baptism changed after reading this chapter? Have you seen it primarily as a water ritual, or as a deeper spiritual immersion into Christ?

2. What does it mean to be "baptized into Christ" rather than just baptized in water?

3. How do Scriptures like Romans 6:3–4 and Galatians 3:27 shape your view?

4. Why is it important to distinguish between John's baptism and the baptism Christ offers?

5. What is the significance of the transition from symbolic water to Spirit and fire?

6. What does it mean that Jesus is our Ark, and how does that truth affect your identity in Him? How does comparing Christ to Noah's ark expand your understanding of baptism and covenant?

7. How do you respond to the truth that Jesus fulfilled all righteousness on your behalf? Does this remove the pressure to "add" to what He's already done?

8. In what ways do believers today still look for symbolic acts to complete salvation? How can we walk in the confidence that "It is finished"?

9. Reflect on Ephesians 4:5: "One Lord, one faith, one baptism." What does this reveal about the unity and simplicity of the New Covenant?

10. If the baptism that saves is spiritual and performed by the Spirit, how can you explain that to someone focused on outward rituals? What Scriptures would help you clarify the difference between shadow and substance?

11. How does understanding your baptism into Christ affect how you see your past, present, and future? Are you living as someone fully immersed in Christ's death, resurrection, and authority?

12. What part of this chapter challenged or encouraged you the most? How will you respond to that in your walk with God?

www.ingramcontent.com/pod-product-compliance
Lightning Source LLC
Chambersburg PA
CBHW060033180426
43196CB00045B/2650